HISTORY OF FUN STUFF

The Colorful Story of COMICS

by Patricia Lakin
illustrated by Rob McClurkan

Ready-to-Read

Simon Spotlight
New York   London   Toronto   Sydney   New Delhi

Hey, kids! Some of the comics mentioned in this book are for grown-ups. Ask your parent or guardian to help you find comics appropriate for your age and reading level.

SIMON SPOTLIGHT
An imprint of Simon & Schuster Children's Publishing Division
1230 Avenue of the Americas, New York, New York 10020
This Simon Spotlight edition September 2016
Text copyright © 2016 by Simon & Schuster, Inc.
Illustrations copyright © 2016 by Rob McClurkan
All rights reserved, including the right of reproduction in whole or in part in any form.
SIMON SPOTLIGHT, READY-TO-READ, and colophon are registered trademarks of Simon & Schuster, Inc.
For information about special discounts for bulk purchases, please contact Simon & Schuster Special Sales at
1-866-506-1949 or business@simonandschuster.com.
Manufactured in the United States of America 0816 LAK
2 4 6 8 10 9 7 5 3 1
Cataloging-in-Publication Data for this title is available from the Library of Congress.
ISBN 978-1-4814-7145-9 (hc)
ISBN 978-1-4814-7144-2 (pbk)
ISBN 978-1-4814-7146-6 (eBook)

CONTENTS

Chapter 1
The Pictures Tell a Story

Imagine it's your bedtime, but instead of sleeping, you're about to read a comic book. You hide under the covers, turn on your flashlight, and flip to the first page. *Wham!* In seconds the pictures and words draw you in. You feel as if you're right in the middle of the action.

When you read comics, you feel like you're transported to another world! Did you know that, in a way, you have cavemen to thank for this?

Have you ever wondered how comic books, graphic novels, and manga came to be? Or who put the funny pages in newspapers? Did you know that history shaped superhero comics? By the time you finish reading this book, you will be a History of Fun Stuff Expert on comics. You may even want to make comics of your own!

What are comics, anyway? At their core, comics are a series of drawings arranged in a specific order to tell a story.

Each drawing in a comic is often placed inside a frame called a "panel," which is usually a square

or rectangle. In between and around the panels, spaces called "gutters" help show the passage of time from one image to the next. Speech bubbles show what characters are thinking or saying. Captions give the time or location, or comment on the story. This kind of storytelling can be traced back to cave paintings of daily life made by humans around seventeen thousand years ago!

In the ancient world, Greeks, Romans, Egyptians, and Mayans carved stories into wide slabs of stone called "friezes" (FREE-zes), which were used to decorate buildings. Mayan friezes even showed what people were saying by adding curvy lines coming from their mouths, similar to speech bubbles in modern comics!

Ancient Romans also carved a story in a spiral around a stone column called Trajan's Column.

In the eleventh century, in Japan, a priest painted picture stories on paper scrolls.

In the fourteenth century, people living in what is now Mexico painted stories in a kind of book called a codex that folds like an accordion! One codex is thirty-six feet long!

Can you imagine if you had to read comics on a building, column, or scroll? How would you share them with a friend?

For centuries, to share a written story with a friend, people had to make a copy by hand. In 1440, a German man named Johannes Gutenberg invented the printing press, and copies of books could be made easily. Without the printing press, comic books might never have been invented!

Then, in 1605, the first weekly newspaper was printed. In 1754 an editorial cartoon was published in an American newspaper for the first time. It was created by Benjamin Franklin! What are editorial cartoons? Similar to a single panel of a comic strip, editorial cartoons pair an exaggerated drawing with a caption to make people laugh, think, or both.

Franklin's cartoon showed a snake cut up into pieces, each representing a part of America, which was still a group of British colonies at that time. Below, a caption said "Join, or Die." Franklin didn't actually want anyone to die, of course. He wanted everyone to work together!

In 1837 a Swiss artist named Rodolphe Töpffer published a book for grown-ups called *The Adventures of Mr. Obadiah Oldbuck* in Switzerland. He used panels of images with captions to tell what were called "picture stories" about a man in love. Töpffer is now known as "the father of the comic strip" because his picture stories were the closest thing to comics the world had ever seen.

In 1895 the first newspaper comic was printed. Richard Outcault's *Hogan's Alley* filled up a whole page of the newspaper and told the story of a scruffy boy named for his long yellow shirt. At first, speech was written on The Yellow Kid's shirt. Then it moved to what are now called speech bubbles. The comic was an instant hit.

Comics helped sell newspapers, so the owner of another paper, William Randolph Hearst, hired Outcault and added *Hogan's Alley* to a new, special newspaper section full of comics. It was nicknamed "the Sunday funnies," or "the funny pages" section.

Readers laughed at the prankster twins in Rudolf Dirk's *The Katzenjammer Kids* and at the goofy pals in Bud Fisher's *Mutt and Jeff*.

The success led Hearst to create King Features Syndicate (SIN-duh-ket). Newspapers around the country paid the syndicate for the rights to print comics, too. Each comic was often limited to a "strip" of up to four panels arranged horizontally. The first modern-day comic strips were born!

CHAPTER 2
Comic Books to the Rescue!

In the early 1930s a man named Max Gaines printed books full of newspaper comics on cheap paper called "pulp" and sold them to large companies . . . to give away for free. Why? Giving away free books helped the companies sell their own products! The idea took off, but when the Great Depression hit, companies couldn't afford to give things away.

Gaines realized people needed entertainment and began to sell comic books at newsstands for just ten cents. They sold out! Then a man named Major

Malcolm Wheeler-Nicholson started publishing books with new comics inside, instead of comics that had already been printed in newspapers. They both hired people from around the country to dream up new comics characters. Eventually, his and Gaines's companies joined together and started a new company that would later become DC Comics.

Two longtime friends began to work at Detective Comics, one of the companies that eventually became part of DC Comics. Jerry Siegel and Joe Shuster had an idea for a comic strip about a shy boy who was secretly a superhero. Superman appeared in June 1938, just when the world needed him.

In Europe a world war was brewing, and the United States joined the fight in 1941. During World War II people craved wholesome, patriotic heroes, and comic book companies had their artists and writers create just that. There was Batman, Captain Marvel, Captain America, and Wonder Woman. Many of their outfits were red, white, and blue like the American flag. The cover of the first Captain America comic book even showed the superhero fighting the Nazi leader, Adolf Hitler. By 1943 comic books were so popular that eighteen million were sold in America each month.

Soon after World War II ended, America began competing with Russia in the Cold War. They competed to see who had the best army and most powerful weapons, and raced to put a human on the moon.

Comic book publishers created new superheroes. Many of these comics turned people's fears into strengths. Science saved the world from evil villains, while usually harmful radiation (ray-dee-AY-shun) turned normal people into superheroes.

In *The Amazing Spider-Man*, created by Steve Ditko and Stan Lee, Peter Parker gained his powers when he was bitten by a radioactive spider. The comic's message, "With great power, there must come great responsibility," spoke to readers and leaders alike. Lee also co-created Iron Man, the Fantastic Four, X-Men, the Hulk, and Thor.

Even though comics often promoted strong morals, some people thought they were too violent. In the 1950s a man named Dr. Fredric Wertham blamed comics for the country's rise in crime by young people.

In 1954 comic book publishers created the Comic Code Authority to give comics a CCA seal of approval if they followed a list of rules and were considered appropriate for kids. Many adults were still worried, so kids in that era often read comic books in secret!

CHAPTER 3
Graphic Novels, Manga, and More

The first comic books were slim booklets meant to entertain readers quickly. They focused on fictional characters and weren't seen as being very serious. Then in the 1970s, Will Eisner made a comic that told a story almost like a novel would, with drawings that were like scenes from a movie.

The panels were drawn from different angles and gave readers a feeling or mood. For example, he drew a dark room covered in shadows except for a bit of light seen through a slightly opened door, and the reader knew to be scared. He also experimented with lettering, or ways of writing the words. He used letters with jagged edges, for example, to show that a character was angry.

Eisner knew his story wasn't right for a newspaper or comic book, so he brought it to a book publisher. When asked to describe his work, a new term popped into Eisner's head. He said, "It's a graphic novel." The word "graphic" (GRAF-ick) means "related to visual arts." Eisner's book, *A Contract with God*, is considered the very first graphic novel and is for grown-up readers.

Some say the only difference between comic books and graphic novels is that comic books are held together with staples, and graphic novels are bound like many standard books. Others say graphic novels have more detailed stories, are longer, and are for older readers.

In Japan another unique form of comics was created: manga (MAHNG-gah). "Manga" is actually the Japanese word for any comic drawing. It means "whimsical" or "playful drawings." Around the world, it came to represent the style of Osamu Tezuka, who is known as the father of manga.

As a child, Tezuka loved Disney movies and Japanese comics, especially the ones influenced by *Hogan's Alley,* Outcault's newspaper comic about the boy with the long yellow shirt. As a grown-up, Tezuka

drew characters with huge eyes and spiked, colorful hair in a style of drawing that was different from anything the comic world had ever seen. One of his many popular characters, Mighty Atom, is known as Astro Boy in the United States. Tezuka even made animated films, called "anime" (AH-nee-may), in Japan.

CHAPTER 4
The Future of Comics

Just as the printing press changed everything in the fifteenth century, computers and the Internet changed how comics were read and made in the late twentieth century and beyond.

Traditionally, comics are drawn in pencil and ink. In newspapers, while the comic strips appear small on the page, they are actually drawn quite large to give artists room to add detail and write text. Then they are shrunk down to fit the size and shape of the strip in the funny pages.

With the invention of computers,

many things changed. People started to experiment with drawing comics and art digitally, on screen, using computer illustration programs.

Computers became more popular. People started reading the news online, advertisers bought fewer newspaper ads, and newspapers started going out of business. Fewer newspapers meant fewer funny pages and comic strips.

In the early twenty-first century, comic creators realized that the Internet gave them a new way to reach readers, even if their comic wasn't printed in a newspaper or comic book. They started posting comics online as what are now called "webcomics."

Unlike in newspaper comic strips, webcomics aren't limited to a certain number of panels. Panels can be arranged vertically (up and down), horizontally (side to side), or any way that tells a story. The panels can also be just about any size!

Even though comics are changing with the times, they aren't going away. Comic book characters are everywhere: on lunch boxes and snack food packaging, in TV shows and movies, and all over the world. Some comics have even been turned into video games!

All comics have one thing in common, whether you read them on paper or onscreen. They all use visual clues.

If one panel is larger than the rest, the action inside it is probably very important.

When your eye moves from one panel to the next, the changes in the art are clues that someone is coming closer to you or moving farther away from you, or that time is passing slowly or quickly.

The shape of a speech balloon or bubble is a clue too. A basic speech bubble "tail" points directly to the character who is speaking. A thought bubble, on the other hand, has little circles leading to the character to show that the words are what the character is thinking. Sometimes thought bubbles even look a bit like clouds. A speech bubble with a jagged or spiky tail or shape means the words inside it are coming from a TV, radio, phone, or other device, or that they are being yelled.

The size and shape of the letters inside speech bubbles and caption boxes are clues to how a character is feeling or how loudly he or she is talking. If the letters are large, the person might be shouting. If the letters are small or lowercase, or the speech bubble is made of dashed lines, the person might be whispering or scared.

There are also symbols called emanata (em-in-AH-tuh), like a lightbulb drawn above a person's head to show that he or she has an idea. It's similar to how symbols were used in ancient Egyptian hieroglyphics!

Has all this made you want to create your own comic strip or graphic novel? Well, grab a blank piece of paper or clear your computer screen and start your own chapter of comic history!

Congratulations! You've come to the end of this book. You are now an official History of Fun Stuff Expert on comics, graphic novels, and more! Next time you see a superhero movie, you can dazzle your friends with facts about how world history played a part in inspiring the creators of the original comics! And when you pick up the funny pages or see a friend reading a graphic novel, remember all the people and inventions who, over thousands of years, made comics possible!

Hey, kids! Now that you're an expert on the history of comics, turn the page to learn even more about comics and some social studies, art, and science, too! Plus, you'll learn the basics to create your own comic!

Comics Around the World

Take a world tour of some popular comics from around the globe!:

Belgium

The Adventures of Tintin

follows a young reporter who, along with his dog, takes on dangerous cases and saves the day.

France

The Adventures of Asterix

follows Asterix and his friend Obélix as they travel and defend their village from Roman occupation. It has been made into many films, video games, and even a theme park!

Zig et Puce was a popular comic that started in 1925 and featured two teens who went on adventures together. It was drawn in a decorative style and was the first French comic to use speech bubbles.

Argentina

Some say the star of *Mafalda*, a comic that began in the 1960s, was like a female version of Charlie Brown from *Peanuts*.

South Africa

Nelson Mandela: The Authorized Comic Book tells the story of the leader's childhood, activism, time in prison, and election.

India

Amar Chitra Katha was created to teach children about mythology and folklore and is known for helping to launch the comic industry in India.

Nagraj, also known as the Snake King, is the star of a bestselling Indian superhero comic of the same name.

Some of these comics are meant for older readers. Head to your local comic book store to find great comics for kids.

The Tools of the Trade

While some comics are illustrated on computers, traditionally, comics are illustrated in pencil and ink. Without the graphite in pencils and the ink used in pens, comics would look very different!

After coming up with an idea, an artist called  a "penciller" sketches out the panels, characters, and action in pencil so it can be changed before moving on to the inking stage. This is because the ink used is permanent and can't be erased!

The "inker" draws over the pencil sketches with black ink using a quill pen, brush, or marker. He or she adds shading, more detail, and other finishing touches to bring the comics to life! Sometimes, after the black ink dries, color ink is added too.

Inking with India Ink

The kind of ink used to draw many comics is often called India ink or Chinese ink.

In ancient China, India, and Egypt, this ink was valued because it didn't smudge when wet and was very, very black.

It was made of fine carbon powder, which was used as a black pigment. Pigments are made of intensely colored particles that are mixed with liquid and used to give color to other materials.

In ancient times carbon powder pigment was made of carbon black or lampblack. To make carbon black, people burned wood, tar, or even animal bones until all that remained was the fine black soot, or carbon black. To make lampblack, they collected the soot from oil lamps. These materials had to be heated to just the right temperature to create pigment. The carbon powder was then pressed into sticks or cakes that could be moistened to use as ink!

Pure Pencils

You might be surprised to learn that the graphite in pencils, the pigment in India ink, and even diamonds are all made from the same element: carbon.

The carbon black used to make India ink actually changes into graphite if it is heated for a long time at five thousand four hundred degrees Fahrenheit (3,500° C). Next time you use a pencil, think about how, in a way, you're writing with a building block of diamonds!

Make Your Own Comics

Have you ever thought about making your own comic strip? There's no time like the present! Start by thinking of a story you want to tell that can be told in a few panels. For example, you could do a comic about a person with a scrawny plant. After he or she waters the plant and puts it in a sunny spot, it sprouts new leaves. When he or she talks to the plant, it grows so much that it fills the panel!

For your comic, imagine the characters and what they might say.

Next, write it all into a script with sentences that tell the story in order. Don't forget to include the characters' dialogue or speech.

Divide your story into four panels. Some of the description in your script can be included in caption boxes. Captions help tell the story by describing where the characters are or when a scene is taking place, and contain phrases like "two weeks later" or "meanwhile, at the grocery store..."

Now do a sketch in pencil. Feel free to erase or change things.

When you are happy with your pencil drawing, draw over the pencil lines in black ink.

Ta-da! You've made a comic strip!

Being an expert on something means you can get an awesome score on a quiz on that subject! Take this

HISTORY OF COMICS QUIZ

to see how much you've learned.

1. Which animal was the focus of Benjamin Franklin's editorial cartoon?

   a. snake
   b. elephant
   c. giraffe

2. Which war influenced the creation of Superman?

   a. Vietnam War
   b. Civil War
   c. World War II

3. Who is known as the father of the comic strip?

   a. Will Eisner
   b. William Randolph Hearst
   c. Rodolphe Töpffer

4. What does the word "manga" mean in Japanese?

   a. whimsical or playful drawing
   b. Japanese comic
   c. anime

5. Which device influenced the comics industry?

   a. printing press
   b. computer
   c. both "a" and "b"

6. Ancient people used images to tell stories on all but which one of these structures?

   a. stone column
   b. stone bridge
   c. stone friezes

7. How much did Max Gaines's comic books cost when they were first sold to the public?

   a. 10 cents
   b. 5 cents
   c. 25 cents

8. How was Will Eisner's graphic novel different from a written novel?

   a. more visual
   b. fictional
   c. shorter

9. What are comics on the Internet called?

   a. digital comics
   b. Internet comics
   c. webcomics

Answers: 1.a 2.c 3.c 4.a 5.c 6.b 7.a 8.a 9.c